McDonnell-Douglas

F-4C/RF-4C PHANTOM II

Ávila Gonzalo and Roberto Yáñez

McDonnell-Douglas

F-4C/RF-4C PHANTOM II

Ávila Gonzalo and Roberto Yáñez

Schiffer Publishing Ltd
4880 Lower Valley Road • Atglen, PA 19310

Originally published in Spanish by Reserva Anticipada, S.L., under the title *McDonnell Douglas F-4C RF-4C Phantom II*
© text by Gonzalo Ávila and Roberto Yáñez
© profile and emblems by Gonzalo Ávila Cruz

English translation by
Omicron Language Solutions, LLC

Library of Congress Control Number: 2014948723

Type set in Frutiger LT Std/Minion Pro

ISBN: 978-0-7643-4371-1
Printed in China

C.12-03 showing its landing gear being retracted shortly after taking off from Torrejón. The building and the large hangar in the background are part of the the 406th Squadron. January 1985 (Lieutenant Colonel Fernando Fernández)

Published by Schiffer Publishing, Ltd.
4880 Lower Valley Road
Atglen, PA 19310
Phone: (610) 593-1777; Fax: (610) 593-2002
E-mail: Info@schifferbooks.com

For our complete selection of fine books on this and related subjects,
please visit our website at www.schifferbooks.com. You may also write for a free catalog.

This book may be purchased from the publisher. Please try your bookstore first.

We are always looking for people to write books on new and related subjects.
If you have an idea for a book, please contact us at proposals@schifferbooks.com.

Schiffer Publishing's titles are available at special discounts for bulk purchases for sales promotions or premiums. Special editions, including personalized covers, corporate imprints, and excerpts can be created in large quantities for special needs. For more information, contact the publisher.

Acknowledgments

The authors wish to dedicate this monograph to the memory of the missing Lieutenant Coronel Fernando Ferrández del Cacho. With his friendship, kindness, and patience, often well beyond all reasonable limits, he made this work possible. Many thanks also go to our friend Commander Terol, to Lieutenant General San Antonio Copero, to Captain Manuel Jorge, to Lieutenant Arnedo, and to Second Lieutenant Pina. Last, but not least, a mention goes to our friends José A. Nebreda, Juan Carlos Pando, Rafael Biedma, Pere Redón, and J.M. Palomino for their crucial contributions.

Introduction

In 1958, when the first drawings and plans of the then-named F4H-1 were published, it was difficult to imagine this aircraft, with its unusual and rather tortured looking shape, becoming one of the most famous planes in aviation history.

Among its characteristic features were the compact fuselage—still a long way from its final shape—designed according to what was called at the time the *transonic area rule*, the *Whitcomb area rule* or, more usually, the *coke bottle*; the dihedral of 12° on the outside of the wings and 23° applied to the horizontal empennage.

And it still lacked the bulky nose that together with the *chin* of some versions gave it its unmistakable appearance. There was little to indicate, thanks to the incredible flexibility of its design, that a spectacular development in the type of tasks originally planned (it was conceived as an interceptor and fighter aircraft) would turn it into, in its guise as the F-4, an effective multirole aircraft.

On the other hand, the engine system was very advanced and this, with the help of som completely innovative air intakes with a variable shape, allowed the aircraft to reach speeds of Mach 2.4—even for today

The Phantom FH-1 was the first Navy (U.S. Marines) carrier-based jet aircraft.

A prototype of the F4H-1, code name *Sageburner*. It achieved a distance record of three kilometers (1.86 miles) flying at 902.77mph at an altitude of 125 feet. From 1968, this has been kept by McDonnell Douglas in St. Louis. (McDonnell Douglas)

F-4E-60-MC (s/n 74-648) in a detachment of the 52 TFW of the USAF in Spangdahlen, Zaragoza, to carry out exercises at the headquarters of the 401st TFTW. The horizontal blue band, almost invisible in the photo, stands for the allocation of this aircraft to the 23 TFS of the 52 TFW. Zaragoza, September 1982. (Pere Redón)

very fast. Lastly, the *progeny* of this strange aircraft, which was divided into almost twenty versions and wore the colors of no less than fifteen air forces, would reach a production figure of more than 5,000 aircraft and would be kept in service for more than forty years, up until the new millennium in 2001.

In support of its impressive historical record, it is enough to say that two world powers—the United Kingdom and Japan—chose the McDonnell aircraft to produce under license.

McDonnell Douglas, manufacturer of the F-4, specialized in fighter aircraft. In particular, its FH-1 *Phantom* was the first turbojet aircraft to operate from an aircraft carrier. The desire to see this success repeated led to McDonell Douglas giving the U.S. Air Force *ground* version, initially the F-110, the nickname *Phantom II*, by which it is known all over the world.

There is quite an exhaustive list of what the F-4 has been used for. The best known versions (the F-4B, F-4C, F-4D, F-4J, F-4K, F-4M, and F-4N) have been used as land and naval fighter-bombers. The F-4E, F-4EJ, and F-4F have been used as multirole fighters. The RF-4C and RF-4E have been used as tactical reconnaissance platforms with cameras and sensors. The F-4G model has taken part in electronic warfare missions. There have even been experimental versions to test different types of wings aimed at improving the maneuverability of the aircraft in combat. In addition to these, there are countries with technological and industrial capacity that have created a large number of their own variants which are too numerous to describe here.

The manufacture of the F-4C and RF-4C models, which are the subjects of this monograph, reached the figures of 583 and 505 aircraft, respectively. The former served in twenty-five wings of the U.S. Air Force, while the photographic variants were in ten. Both of them played fundamental roles in the long conflict in Vietnam, during which their equipment and missions developed at the same time as their defense and enemy attack systems. Their legendary ability to adapt really began during this bloody war, from the initial fighter, bombing, and machine gun missions, which were immediately followed by the suppression of defenses, planting sound and vibration recorder sensors to control enemy movement, aerial superiority, and many other tasks. On the other hand, the high rate of accidents produced by the violent maneuvers they had to perform to avoid lethal Vietnamese SAMs were the origin for the adoption of slats. Similarly, the debatable effectiveness of the cannon carrying pods in combat with the MiG gave rise to the fitting of internal cannons.

The more modern versions, which also took part in the Vietnam war, were also fully involved in many other conflicts, such as the interminable problems in the Middle East and the Iran-Iraq war.

In the book of world records, the *Phantom* has more than a few entries. The first, for height, was reached in December 1959 (30000m - 9,842ft), and the last, so as not to make this an excessively long list, was in November 1961, when it reached a speed of 1,980km/h (1,230mph) in a circuit of 25km (15.53 miles). Some of these records lasted many years before they were broken.

This is a summary of this legendary aircraft that, as someone once said, is *double* in many senses: the crew, the engine, the maximum Mach number, the possibility to refuel while in the air, and even the name itself: *Phantom II*.

The F-4Cs were assigned to the 121st Squadron in the same order as their registration numbers in the first months of service in the Air Force. They did not yet use the emblem of the Ala. (CECAF)

The Phantom II in Spain

The operational life of the F-4C Phantom II in Spain began in the middle of June 1971, when the first aircraft of this type arrived in Torrejón to replace the F/TF-104G and F-86F. As a result of the renewal of and changes to the U.S.-Spain agreement signed by both parties on August 6, 1970 for a period of five years, Spain received a number of surplus F-4Cs from the U.S. Air Force.

The Air Force initially wanted the F-4E, but due to budgetary limitations it had to accept the F-4C. Curiously, some specialist magazines of the period stated the Phantom delivered to Spain came from the U.S. Navy.

Together with the 36 Phantom aircraft at that time called the F-4C(S), three Boeing KC-97L tankers and two C-97 tankers arrived. The cost of the operation rose to 7,200 million *pesetas* (59,832,000 USD). Half was financed by a loan from the U.S. Ex-Imbank and the rest by funds made available by the Spanish government.

This is not the place to analyze the circumstances in which the renewal of the agreement with the USA took place. However, from the condition of the material which was received, it can be assumed that the reasons for the Spanish government accepting it are quite unclear.

The agreement was never known for its generosity, but on this occasion and viewed from today's perspective, the transactions reached truly offensive proportions.

Despite being second hand aircraft, many of which had taken part in the Vietnam war, the F-4C gave the Spanish Air Force its largest fighting capacity in its history. They were the most powerful aircraft they had ever had and very soon the black vapor trails of their two J79-GE-15s with 7,720kg (17,900lb) thrust grew to be familiar sights. *When you see two black vapor trails in the distance, you can be sure that there is a Phantom in front of them.* The compact shape of the aircraft earned it the nickname *flying cupboard* from the pilots and maintenance staff.

To familiarize themselves with the new aircraft, a group of eight men chosen from amongst those who had piloted the F-104G and the F-86F left for Davis Monthan AFB, Arizona, in February 1971, and joined the 4453 CCTW (Combat Crew Training Wing). Once their training was finished and they had returned to Spain, they acted as instructors for their colleagues.

Together with the aircraft, a flight procedures trainer was also acquired. It was not really a simulator, as it had two seats: one for the pilot and one for the officer in

▲ C.12-25 at an Open Day during the Day of Friendship clearly shows the consequences of the recent change of allocation for each aquadron of Ala 12. There was the possibility that initially more than 36 aircraft would arrive. Torrejón, 6-17-1973. (J. A. Nebreda)

▲ C.12-15, an F-4C of 121 Squadron, with the nose cone open to allow access for the AN/APQ-100 radar, an element very sensitive to moisture. Torrejón, 1-31-1974. (J. A. Nebreda)

Three Boeing KC-97L tankers were assigned to the 123rd Squadron. One of them was TK.1-1/123-01. They provided in-flight refueling for the Phantoms for almost four years. Fortunately, TK.1-3 has been kept at the Air Museum in Cuatro Vientos. It is worth mentioning the background presence of two F-104Gs of the JG-74, probably en route to Portugal. Torrejón, 1-31-1974. (J. A. Nebreda)

arms with all the instruments, including the flight controls. It was installed in Torrejón, allowing for future crews to familiarize themselves with the controls quickly.

Shortly afterwards, the first Phantom IIs began to arrive at CASA-Getafe for PDM (Programmed Depot Maintenance); from 1967, the Spanish company carried out the Mod/IRAN on the USAFE (United States Air Force in Europe) F-4 aircraft. The Spanish F-4Cs were amongst those that had less time in use in the 81 TFW (Tactical Fighter Wing) of the USAFE and were flown from their British base in Bentwaters to Getafe by pilots from that unit. The first (F-4C-25-MC 64-895) arrived at CASA on February 23, 1971 and stayed there for almost nine months. The PDM lasted between 30 and 45 days, meaning this aircraft (and probably others) received a complete Mod/IRAN on arrival.

The next aircraft (the Air Force C-12) landed in Torrejón in the middle of June 1971 and joined the 121st Squadron. The last of the thirty-six Phantoms of the 81 TFW arrived in August 1972.

Previously, on March 25th, Ala 12 was born, with its first squadron (the 104th) fitted with the F/TF-104G assigned to it on the 27th of the same month. Four days later, the 121st Squadron—radio code *Poker*—

which had replaced the 201st and was fitted with the F-86F, became the second part of the Wing, and at this point the 104th went over to the 122nd Squadron, radio code *Tennis*. Ala 12 therefore became a mixed F-104/F-4 unit until May 31, 1972, when all the Starfighters, apart from one of the two-seaters bought by the Spanish government, were returned to the USAF.

CASA delivered two aircraft a month until the Air Force had taken delivery of 28 Phantoms, which was enough to start fitting out another squadron; this was due to the transfer from the United Kingdom being fairly quick.

The F-4C, which had been assigned to the 121st Squadron with numbers in line with those of their registrations, began to be divided into two groups: those with odd-numbered registrations stayed in the 121st, while those with even numbers went to the 122nd. The number of crew members that had completed Instruction Plan No. 1 was also high. Because of this, the 122nd Squadron was disbanded and recreated on May 31, 1972, with F-4C aircraft. Therefore,

It seems that in Torrejón they were expecting a higher number of F-4Cs, approximately 20 aircraft per squadron. When the 122nd Squadron was created, a distinctive feature of the 121st was the outlined target of the unit registration number. C.12-29/121-15 in Torrejón, February 1974. (J. A. Nebreda)

"If you see two black vapor trails in the distance, there is a Phantom in front of them." A good illustration of this can be seen in this photo of two C.12s landing in Torrejón, January 1974. (B. A. de Torrejón)

Ala 12 consisted of two squadrons of Phantom IIs, each with 18 aircraft, plus a third squadron for in-flight refueling shortly to be formed from three KC-97Ls.

The introduction of the Phantom into service was not as easy as hoped due to the deterioration of the aircraft during operations in Vietnam. On the other hand, the acquisition of spare parts was slow and costly. Therefore, the command of Ala 12 had to create and organize a Maintenance Group on its own base. By working very hard, it was soon able to offer a reasonable number of operational aircraft on a daily basis. First and second grade repairs were carried out on the base and third grades (Mod/IRAN) took place at CASA-Getafe.

In September 1973, the 401st TFW (part of the 16th Air Force of the USAFE in Torrejón) rather surprisingly saw its F-4Es replaced by F-4Cs, and both tenants of the base started to use the same version. Spanish maintenance personnel made the best possible use of the situation and borrowed spare parts. When the rather slow process of official requests began to arrive, the Spanish technicians gave them back to their neighbors. Thanks to this unofficial system, a very reasonable degree of aircraft availability was obtained over the first period.

▲ Parking area in Torrejón. The closest aircraft (C.12-19) has its nose open to allow access to the radar antenna, something that caused a number of problems for maintenance services. In the background is TK.1-3/123-03. The KC-97Ls never had their registrations painted. Torrejón, February 1974. (Gonzalo Ávila)

▲ Up on the fin of the left air inlet, J. A. Nebreda pays attention to the explanations given by the pilot regarding the distribution of the rear cabin. The registration plate of this aircraft (C.12-33/122-16) has undergone some variations. Until 1977, Ala 12, which succeeded Ala 16, had aerial defense as its main mission. Torrejón, February 1974. (Gonzalo Ávila)

On a cold winter morning, the take-off of an F-4C demonstrates a great feeling of power with a thundering roar. Torrejón, 1978. (B. A. de Torrejón)

Operational Status of the F-4C

Ala 12 began the adaptation of the Phantom II at the beginning of 1972 and reached total operational status in 1973. The first public appearance of the F-4C took place on April 5, 1972, when a formation of eight aircraft from the 121st Squadron flew over the crowd at Tablada aerodrome in an aerial exhibition called *Mirlo* (Blackbird). This was the nickname of the then Air Force Minister during the civil war.

The F-4C had been built in the mid-sixties, and it had not been possible to verify the flight hours of the aircraft on their arrival in Spain, despite their PDMs. Nonetheless, when most of them began to pass the Mod/IRAN at the end of 1974, the opportunity was taken to improve their Westinghouse APQ-100 radar equipment and Litton ASN-48 inertial navigation system. They were also able to solve the problems caused by humidity and condensation on the radar equipment situated in the nose of the aircraft, a defect which had already shown up in Vietnam. Shortly afterwards, they began to take part in different exercises, both inside and outside Spanish air space: *Red Eye*, with units from the *Armée del l'Air*, USAF, Portuguese ForÁa, and the AAA units operated by the Army; *Poop-Deck* and *Cruiser*, with the U.S. Navy, USAF, and the Spanish Army and Navy; and *Navipar*, *Datex*, and *Ejedan* in support of the Spanish Navy and others.

In the middle of 1974, it was rumored that 100 F-4C surplus aircraft were going to be acquired from the USAF, and shortly afterwards, the F-4Es were to be reduced to 35 or 40. In the end, none of this happened. In February 1978, it was made public that *FACA* planned to purchase 144 fighter aircraft and, of lesser importance, defense aircraft to replace the F-4C and F-5. This would force the Phantom to fly for twelve more years.

Retirement of the TK.1

After almost four years and more than 1,000 flight hours, during which time around 1,000,000 liters (264,172 gallons) of JP4 were supplied day and night, the three aircraft whose acquisition was temporary were retired in mid-1976. Even the J47-GE-25 auxiliary turbojets were disconnected to avoid maintenance. The retirement of the KC-97L meant the end of in-flight refueling for the Phantom, as the system used by the new KC-130H was not compatible with the dorsal tanks on the F-4C.

▲ F-4C 64-892 (future C.12-39) still with the decoration of the USAF shortly after joining the Air Force. Torrejón, 9-8-1978. (J. A. Nebreda)

▲ Before leaving on a mission, an ECM AN/ALQ-71 mechanism can be seen on C.12-06 in the front right hand niche designed for housing AIM-7E Sparrow missiles. On the left it is carrying an ECM AN/ALQ-72 mechanism. Torrejón, 9-8-1978. (J. A. Nebreda)

These aging KC-97Ls—ex-107 ARG, 136 ARS, and New York ANG—together with the two C-97s which were used for spare parts, arrived in May 1972. With these aircraft (called here the TK.1), the 123rd Squadron, also known as the 123-K Squadron, was formed on August 8, 1972, providing the Ala with suitable in-flight refueling. The first in-flight refueling took place in mid-July 1972, when two F-4Cs were refueled over the Mediterranean.

By that time, four Phantoms had been lost. Three of them—C.12-05 (26.11.1973), C.12-25 (14.02.1975), and C.12-21 (14.10.1977)—were destroyed and the fourth (C.12-01) was retired due to a fire in its electrical system that occurred in Torrejón in July 1978. Later, this aircraft went to the Specialists School in León to be used as a training unit. Three pilots and three officers in arms died in the accidents. The main cause was identified as an uncontrollable reaction in the stalls. The F-4C did not have leading edge slats (only flaps), and when a pilot pulled the lever at low speed and high loads at less than 3,000m (9,843ft)—especially when these were fitted in the centerline—the aircraft entered a terrible stall, followed almost inevitably by an irrecoverable spin. It was an axe type spin, during which the pilots knew the F-4C was lost.

C.12-14/122-07 carrying a RMU-10/A target towing mechanism under its left side. The 2,270 liter (599.67 gallon) tank is situated in the centerline and there are two 1,400 (369.8 gallon) underwing tanks, each one giving enough autonomy for the air-to-air shooting mission at LED-26, to the south of Ibiza. Torrejón, 10-1-1978. (Gonzalo Ávila)

In some aircraft, such C.12-26/122-13, the black paint of the nose began to deteriorate, leaving the fiberglass of the original construction uncovered. This earned them the nickname *lepers* among the pilots and mechanics. Under its left side it is carrying a target towing mechanism. Torrejón, 9-8-1978. (J. A. Nebreda)

TJ 63-492 showing the tip of its blue and white checkered fin, indicating that the aircraft belonged to the 612 TFS of the 401 TFW. The similarities in the version used by this unit and that used by Ala 12 during this period meant that Spanish maintenance services had the possibility of obtaining spare parts more quickly. Torrejón, 10-1-1978. (J. A. Nebreda)

To cover the lost aircraft, four F-4Cs offered by the USAF were purchased in 1978, including the 58 TFTW, Luke AFB, and Arizona. They arrived in Torrejón between July and August 1978 still with the emblems of the USAF. They were distributed between the 121st and 122nd Squadrons (from then on the aircraft belonged to Maintenance and not, as previously, to the operative Squadrons) after having only one PDM in CASA-Getafe. This inspection was not sufficient and frequent breakdowns meant that the Mod/IRAN had to be carried out soon.

The Tactical Reconnaissance RF-4Cs

At the same time, four RF-4Cs of the 363 TRW, Shaw AFB, South Carolina, arrived as part of the *Peace Alfa II* Program. Called CR.12s, they provided the day and night tactical reconnaissance lacking for the Air Force, as it only had eighteen RF-5As.

C.12-07/121-04 begin its taxi for take-off at Manises air base. Under its left side it is carrying a target towing mechanism for air-to-air shooting practice, November 1984. (Pere Redón)

At the beginning, a smaller division was formed by the RF-4C inside the 122nd Squadron (a squadron is usually divided up administratively into smaller divisions) and was initially often used for civilian missions: agronomy, cartography, and archeology amongst others. All the same, the crew members were able to familiarize themselves with the cameras, optical and electronic sensors, etc.

The main avionics of the RF-4C consisted of an APQ-99 terrain-following forward looking radar, a Litton ASN-56 inertial navigation system, a SLAR APQ-102 that made maps, and AN/AAS-18A infrared detector equipment able to record images. The photographic equipment was formed of KA-56 panoramic low altitude cameras and panoramic high altitude and Hycon KS-87 cameras for day and night use for low and high altitude. It also had a flash cartridge discharger in the rear of the fuselage for night operations.

The F-4C attended most of the Air Force aerial demonstrations. Normally the solo was carried out by hair raising flyovers right over the spectators at low altitude and high speed. The proverbial trails of black vapor characteristic of the J79-GE-15 can be seen. Cuatro Vientos, April 1988. (Gonzalo Ávila)

Modernization of infrastructures

Until 1977, the Phantoms of Ala 12 integrated into the Defense Command; together with the Mirage IIIEE/DE of Ala 11 in Manises and the Mirage F1CE/BE of Ala 14 in Los Llanos, they had a main mission to be ready for interception and to carry out quick reaction alert (QRA) operations, although they also carried out tactical missions. At this time, the Defense Command worked with a manually operated system that was going to be automated as part of the *Combat Grande* project. With this they were following the modernization and strengthening of seven early warning long-range radar sites and the microwave communications network. The new semi-automatic system went into service in October 1977, and included a COC (Combat Operations Center) and territorial SOCs (Security Operation Centers). In the COC, a Hughes M5118M computer processed all of the information sent by the long range immediate alert stations known as *Escuadrones de Vigilancia Aérea* (Air Vigilance Squadrons, or EVA).

Throughout 1973, the change in the allocation of the two squadrons of Ala 12 took place. In September1980, this was obvious when looking at C.12-10/122-05. The grayish shade of the last three digits (2-05) shows that it has been repainted. Its first serial number was 121-10. Torrejón, 9-17-1980. (Gonzalo Ávila)

In January 1978, the Ministry of Air disappeared and the Air Force joined with the other two arms to make a single Ministry of Defense. Its new structure was composed of three high level groups, one of which was the Air Force, made up of four subordinate Aerial Commands: MACOM (Aerial Combat Command), MATAC (Tactical Aerial Command), MATRA (Transport Aerial Command), and MACAN (Canarian Aerial Command).

MACOM succeeded the Defense Command, keeping Alas 11, 12, and 14 and the Alert and Control Wing stationed at Torrejón, in charge of COC and situated in an underground center on this base.

At the beginning, the C.12 *Charlie* carried the Sidewinder AIM-9B on interception missions, but from 1978, all the MACOM fighter aircraft received the more modern Sidewinder AIM-9J and later the L model. They could also carry four Sparrow III AIM-7E, and as they did not have internal cannons, they could hang up to three SUU-16/A (Vulpods) containers with a 20mm Vulcan cannon for air-to-air and air-to-land shooting practice. However, these weapons, one of which was often carried in the centerline in shooting exercises, were not to the pilots' taste, due to their considerable parasitic resistance, the notable deterioration of the provision of

Shortly after being delivered to Ala 12, C.12-40 aborted its take-off due to fuel leaking from the tank on the left wing, an almost chronic problem on the first F-4C. The white stencils reveal that the Air Force colors had still not been applied. Note the luminous bands for formation flights. Torrejón, 9-8-1978. (Gonzalo Ávila)

the aircraft, and the relative dispersion of the missiles. On the other hand, the mixed SUU-20/A dispensers with 6 BE-11 practice bombs and 4 2.75-inch rockets were highly rated for air-to-land shooting. These were carried out in Caudé and Bárdenas Reales, which in a relatively good time guaranteed a high rate of satisfactory missions.

The air-to-air shooting practices were carried out on LED-26, a restricted aerial zone over the sea to the south of the island of Ibiza. In these exercises, both the C.12 and the C.9 (SF/SRF-5As) were able to tow targets. The type they used most often was a version of the TDU-10/B made under license in Spain, although there was considerable resistance in Ala 12 to using the Phantom for towing targets.

To acquire necessary experience in aerial defense, the training for air combat was soon tackled. Participating in this were other aircraft from MACOM—the Mirage IIIEE and later the F.1CE—allowing for a certain degree of variation. The Phantom II showed a good combination of high speed and maneuverability, meaning it was not difficult for it to overtake the two French aircraft in certain areas of aerial combat. In addition, the C.12 was often able to undertake combat training with its brothers from the 401st TFW.

During 1978, some quite basic (and antiquated) ECM (Electronic Countermeasure) equipment was delivered to Ala 12, consisting of AN/ALQ-72 and -71 jamming pods that allowed the Spanish pilots to become familiar with these mechanisms. By then, the C.12 of the Ala had reached over 20,000 flight hours.

In June 1979, the F-4C went outside of Spain for the first time, when C.12-40 visited the International Air Tattoo. In Ala 12, some pilots had complained that in their unit no visits to other countries had taken place, such as those undertaken by Ala 11. However, in May 1982, Spain was admitted as the sixteenth member of NATO, even though its integration was not complete. This meant that the Air Force was able to participate normally in the Coalition exercises and Ala 12 joined the Squadron Exchange program. Its missions took on a more offensive character.

► This view of the transfer of C.12-09/121.05 shows its unmistakable naval origins due to its capacity to retract the outside fins. Right on the end of the trailing edge of the stabilizer, the mouth of the fuel tube can be seen. Manises air base, November 1984. (Pere Redón)

▼ C.12-27/121-14 and C.12-23/121-12 in one of the warning hangars at Torrejón air base, ready for an interception mission, November 1984. (Pere Redón)

The USAF had more than 500 RF-4Cs in service. 68-564, a RF-4C-38-MC, appears with the colors of the 38 TRS 26 TRW, based in Zweibrücken. It belonged to a series of 15 aircraft that were more modern than those delivered to the Air Force. (Gonzalo Ávila)

The following year, a squadron of Ala 12 took part in its first exchange. The foreign unit was JG 74 *Mölders* of the *Luftwaffe*, from the Neuburg base. This was followed by the 1st Group of the Canadian Air Force (CAF), Baden Sollingen; in October 1983, JBG 34, Hopstein; in 1984, 337 Mira Phantasma, Larissa, of the *Polemiki Aeroporia*; in 1985, JBG 41, Husum; in 1986, the 10e Wing, Kleine Brogel, of the Belgian Force *Aeriénne*; and in 1987, JG 71 *Richthofen*, Wittmundhafen.

The great war load capacity of the Phantom allowed for and favored its frequent use in the development and testing of the most modern laser guided bombs built in Spain. At the end of November 1983, a large scale bombing and real shooting practice took place at Las Bárdenas Reales firing range. An environment had been created there that was very similar to that which could be found on an actual enemy aerial base: control tower, hangars, buildings, landing strip with stationary aircraft, vehicles, fuel tanks, and SAM batteries. In this exercise CR.12 and C.12 were used. The former was used for tactical reconnaissance, mainly for verification and evaluation of the attacks, while the latter was used for weapons. With the support of two F-5s that acted as target setters, C.12 used two laser guided GBU-10 bombs for the first time in Spain.

An unusual picture. Faced with a lack of operational Phantoms, some were taken from CASA-Getafe with just a finish of green primer, the roundels, registration plates, and unit serial number. In this case, it is C.12-30/122-15 of Commander Ferrández del Cacho, Chief of the Maintenance Squadron of Ala 12. Its name appears painted in white on the left side of the aircraft. Getafe, 9-11-1985. (CASA, J. M. Palomino)

At the beginning of the 1980s, the Maintenance Squadron of Ala 12 was still maintaining daily availability levels of close to 55%, with an average of twenty aircraft, which was surprising, given the age of the F-4C and the growing difficulty of obtaining expensive spare parts from McDonnell.

In March 1985, the F-4C had reached almost 53,000 flight hours in 34,400 outings and the RF-4C had 2,580 hours in 1,670 outings. During these outings, four lost F-4Cs and a lost crew must be counted; the other three saved themselves by jumping out. These were C.12-13 (5/7/1979), C.12-35 (4/25/1983), C.12-24 (5/4/1984), and C.12-06 (2/7/1985).

The end of the F-4C seemed to be fast approaching, but fitted with efficient laser guided bombs and packets of chaff situated inside the air brakes, the old Phantom still packed a powerful punch. At this time, they were still carrying out simulated combat with their neighbors, the F-16s of the 401 TFW. However, the difficulties involved in obtaining spare parts were becoming chronic, meaning that the number of non-operational aircraft increased spectacularly.

A formation of three F-4Cs heading to Las Bárdenas firing range. Together with the SUU-16/A ventral pod with a 20mm Vulcan cannon, they carry SUU-20/A underwing dispensers in one of the internal wing supports. This photo from January 1985 indicates that the aircraft has recently undergone an inspection based on the condition of the camouflage. (Fernando Ferrández)

Some F-4Cs in a situation AOCP (Aircraft Out of Commission for Parts) and also in need of a mod/IRAN had to be transferred to CASA-Getafe by the Air Force CH-47C Chinook, acting as a flying crane. Despite this, most of the C.12s could not be retired, even if there were still four years until the EF-18 arrived. Even C.12-01, preserved in León, was emptied for spare parts. Its left side, for example, was removed and fitted to another damaged model, then replaced by one made of wood.

At the end of fall 1985, the operational capacity of Ala 12 had decreased to alarming levels. Due to this, pilots from the unit had to take back some recently checked C.12s from CASA-Getafe, even some which had not yet had their camouflage applied. This meant some F-4Cs appeared in Torrejón with their apple green color primer, the first finish applied in the factory. Faced with this situation, maintenance considered the possibility of asking the U.S. to exchange an F-4C that had flown into Torrejón for USAF combat repair team practice for a damaged C.12, an idea that was ultimately rejected. An alternative idea considered was to contact some particular Americans who had hold of stocks of USAF spare parts; however, the purchase prices quickly dissuaded supporters of this idea.

In the first two weeks of April 1986, the F-4C carried out some rare air-to-land night attack exercises at Las Bárdenas firing range. For these, they carried out bombing in pairs: one of the aircraft launched flares and the other discharged the bombs visually. These exercises coincided with the Libyan crisis and later attacks by the USAF on its targets.

In August and September 1987, the F-4Cs of Ala 12 were still playing an important role, carrying out missions against naval formations during the maritime invasion of the ZIEE (Spanish Zone of Strategic Interest) in the south Atlantic by an enemy convoy in the NATO *Ocean Safari* exercise.

► A formation of four F-4Cs of Ala 12 comes down to land at Zaragoza air base, after some exercises at Bardenas Reales firing range, May 1982. (Pere Redón)

▼ C.12-08/121-08 receives final instructions before leaving for Torrejón. Manises air base, November 1984. (Pere Redón)

When the first EF-18s arrived in Torrejón in March 1989, six F-4Cs stayed in service because they still had some valid flight hours left. Shortly afterwards, C.12-20 was retired when these came to an end, but Ala 12 kept the other five for training the new crews of the 123rd Squadron and for Ala 54 to use in aerial practice exercises for different types of bombs. Torrejón, 5-10-1989. (Gonzalo Ávila)

In 1988, the avionics of the first four RF-4Cs were very antiquated and the general condition of the aircraft was deteriorating rapidly. Finally, due to the scarcity of the ever more burdensome spare parts, Command Ala 12 HQ had to order the "cannibalization" of some aircraft in AOCP for pieces to keep the rest of the planes in the air.

In April 1986, the Air Force committee visited Strasburg to assess the capacity of the Mirage F.1CRs of Escadron 2/33. According to some sources, the Air Force ordered around six of the armed reconnaissance aircraft to assign them full time to Ala 14, but lack of funds finally led to the request being cancelled.

The only thing left was to wait for the arrival of the EF-18 to incorporate the ATARS reconnaissance pods. However, the development of these mechanisms was delayed, and as a temporary measure, eight new surplus RF-4Cs from the ANG were acquired at low cost, making up the 123rd Squadron of Ala 12. Shortly afterwards, three of the first four RF-4Cs, curiously enough manufactured after those which had recently arrived, were withdrawn and used for spare parts.

Ala 12 Created at the same time as Ala de Caza no. 6, with its base in Torrejón, the head of the menacing black cat can be seen for the first time on the right side of the nose of this F-86F. It was later inherited by F/TF-104G, and in 1973, it began to appear on the fins of the F-4C. Nowadays, they are used by the EF-18 and RF-4C of Ala 12. The motto "Don't try to find three paws" (when the cat has four) comes from a Spanish saying and here means that members of the military forces should obey orders without questioning them. The cat is the symbol of the city of Madrid, which is near the Torrejón base.

Returning from an air-to-land shooting exercise at Caudé firing range, C.12-03 begins a gentle turn on its approach to Torrejón de Ardoz. The pod under the fuselage, containing a Vulcan cannon, is very visible. January 1985. (Fernando Ferrández)

121st Squadron The first unofficial emblem of the 121st Squadron, seen on the pilots' flight overalls. It symbolizes the aerial surveillance mission of the F-4Cs assigned to the Aerial Defense Command.

121st Squadron Later on, the first emblem of the 121st Squadron became official, then went on to become part of the flight overalls of the pilots of the unit. It seems there was an attempt to devise another one similar to this with a blue background for the 122nd Squadron.

121st Squadron In the spring of 1986, new emblems were created for the 121st and 122nd Squadrons. The emblem of the 121st Squadron reflected its radio code *Poker*. When refitted with EF-18s, the squadron inherited it.

122 Squadron The emblem of the 122nd Squadron was created in 1986. Initially, this unit did not have one, because its pilots claimed that of the black cat as its own. The motto *De lo dicho... nada!* (Of what's been said … nothing!) is a very common phrase, meaning that after having discussed the missions of the day at length in the briefing beforehand, everything can change in the end. The pirate represents the steep climb of some of its pilots when flying at a very low altitude, which in Air Force slang is known as *piratear* (pirating). The racket symbolizes the unit's radio code *Tennis*. Just like the 121st Squadron, the emblem is still used for the EF-18.

In January 1989, eight new RF-4Cs arrived. CR.12-42 was the only one from 1978 which joined them because it had just passed a PDM and still had 400 valid flight hours. When it was retired a year and a half later, the Maintenance Squadron used it for spare parts. It is currently in the Air Force Museum. Torrejón, 10-30-1990. (Gonzalo Ávila)

New RF-4C

The eight aircraft that came from the 165 TRS of the 123 TRW, Kentucky ANG, arrived at Torrejón January 10 and 11, 1989, manned by members of the ANG. The new 123rd Squadron (radio code Titan) was unofficially reactivated (it seems that there is no official date of its creation) with a very different mission from its previous one: to provide Ala 12 with considerable full time tactical reconnaissance capacity.

These RF-4Cs incorporated various improvements, including an AN/AAD-5 high resolution infrared line scanner and sensor; Have Quick frequency hopping radio equipment, jamming enemy communications with its frequencies (they are the only Air Force aircraft that have this effective ECCM system); a cell with less flight hours; J79-GE-15E low-smoke emission engines; high speed jettisonable tanks; and an improved version of the AN/ARQ 25 and 26 warning and guidance systems. The set of camera equipment was similar to that of the first four RF-4Cs.

Three of the eight RF-4Cs (ex 123 TRW 165 TRS, Kentucky ANG, Louisville AFB) arrived with the *Europa 1* camouflage in three shades. They had been substantially modernized and allowed Ala 12 to dispense with three of the first four aircraft of this type that it had for eleven years. CR.12-49 was one of these. Torrejón, 5-10-1989. (Gonzalo Ávila)

CR.12-44 is just about to commence the day's operations. At the beginning, most of them were of a civilian nature, such as agricultural and cartographic services. These outings provided the crew of Ala 12 with valuable experience in tactical reconnaissance, helping them to get to know the various somewhat antiquated features of their equipment. Torrejón, 9-17-1980. (Gonzalo Ávila)

The End of the F-4C

March 28, 1989, was the date planned for the arrival of the first EF-18 for Ala 12, and on February 20th, all the F-4Cs were retired except six: C.12-09, -10, -14, -19, -20, and -37. Shortly afterwards C.12-20 was also withdrawn for being over hours. The rest still had a valuable number of structural flight hours after the last mod/IRAN.

CR.12-42, which was in a PDM at that time, joined with the five survivors and the personnel of the 123rd Squadron used them, despite not being assigned to that unit, for the conversion of new pilots and arms operators, and to tow targets on occasion.

During those years, the Spanish Air Force, like many other air forces, suffered from a significant shortage of flight personnel due to people leaving for the civil sector, where salaries were higher. When delivery was taken of the eight RF-4Cs, for example, there was only one pilot and one arms operator for these aircraft.

First view of the refueling probe that was fitted in the RF-4C by a group of Israeli technicians to increase its operational radius. It is very similar to that of the F-4E of the IDFAF. They are currently the only aircraft able to carry out in-flight refueling by means of two different systems. Los Llanos, 6-18-1995. (J. A. Nebreda)

CR.12-59/12-50: one of the eight RF-4Cs delivered to Ala 12 at the beginning of 1989, after which time the insignias of the Air Force and the unit were applied. Torrejón, 5-10-1989. (Gonzalo Ávila)

A part of the training for crews of the 123rd Squadron is carried out at low altitude. This is CR.12-45, showing the type of camouflage called *Europa 1*. (Air Force press office)

The Flight Exercise Group of Ala 54—previously the 406th Squadron—also operated the five F-4Cs in various exercises of armament manufactured in Spain, designed nationally or under license. After more than a year and a half of use by the 123rd Squadron, CR-12-42 was retired and the Maintenance Squadron took charge of the aircraft and used it for repairs to some of the F-4C systems. After a time, it was sent to the Air Museum in Cuatro Vientos.

Finally, on March 11, 1991, the operational parts of the five C.12s and CR.12-42 were withdrawn. It was the farewell of the F-4C in Spain, whose last appearance in public took place in Zaragoza on September 19, 1988, with the intervention of C.12-03, -14, -15, -18, -29, and -39.

The numerous admirers of the *flying cupboard* would no longer see its impressive public displays. The solo demonstrations, especially fly overs at thunderous low altitude and high speed, were unforgettable. Fortunately, it was still to be many more years before these aircraft, in their more stylized RF-4C version, would abandon the Spanish skies. The pilots of the old *Charlie*, who felt great affection for the aircraft, also missed being able to fly it again, even though they admitted that it was not suitable for novices, as there were areas that required very skillful reactions. The terrible

123rd Squadron One of the authors of this monograph designed the emblem in March 1989, in response to a request from the pilots of the 123rd Squadron. The eagle is a very representative animal for a tactical reconnaissance unit: it has very sharp eyesight and is very aggressive (the RF-4Cs use it today as a defense weapon). The black and white eagles, and the sun, moon, and the stars signify the capacity of the unit to operate both day and night. The motto *Mille ambulat oculis* has a double meaning, because the main mission of the squadron is to see everything and also to operate with great precision, because most of its missions are carried out at low and very low altitudes.

axe turns at low altitude and reduced speed and the difficulty of flying in formation were two oft-remembered aspects.

The incorporation of external luminous bands was very well received, as the strange dihedral of the wings of the Phantom caused disorientation and abnormal feelings, especially in formations in the clouds, which were dangerous for the crew members, who did not have a reliable visual reference. The flight hours undertaken by C.12 in Spain reached 69,772.15 hours and at the end of 1999, the RF-4C had flown 18,725.20 hours.

To mark eighteen years in the Air Force, on June 1, 1991 (the official retirement of the last F-4C together with the first three RF-4Cs had taken place on March 11th), an F-4C without all the internal equipment was erected as a monument atop a metal post in a small square at Torrejón. Curiously,

Formation of CR.12-52 of the 123rd Squadron with a German RF-4E from the 511 I/AG 51 Staffel in a squadron exchange near Freiburg, summer 1990. (*Revista de Aeronáutica y Astronaútica*)

After returning from a reconnaissance mission, specialist personnel extract the film from the cameras of CR.12-51. The gray color scheme is recent and does not yet have the emblem of the fierce Torrejón cat. Torrejón, November 1990. (José Terol)

on this F-4C—the real C.12-02—the serial number C.12-01 had been painted and the code 12-01, equally symbolic, was put on the body.

Up until now, five aircraft have been preserved: C.12-37 and CR.12-42 are in the Air Museum in Cuatro Vientos; two are in Torrejón; C.12-19 is in the Museum of Ala 12, as well as C.12-02; and the fifth is in León. Most of the fleet of retired F/RF-4Cs is in the open air in areas of Torrejón, waiting for an unknown destination. For some time, there were unfounded rumors they would be sold to Turkey, but this has not materialized. Some were moved to Las Bárdenas firing range. The former predators have become the prey.

New Camouflage and Some Improvements

In 1990, a directive from the Air Force ordered that the majority of operational aircraft be low visibility gray. In addition, at the beginning of 1991, it was announced that the RF-4Cs were being fitted with an in-flight fueling system. This modification was carried out at Torrejón by Israeli technicians and included a fixed detachable arm to communicate with the No. 2 tank of the fuselage, very similar to that carried by the F-4E of the IDFAF. In practice it is never detached.

After a longer period of time than expected, in December 1991, Ala 12 took delivery of the first RF-4C (CR.12-45) with the new gray covering on the upper surfaces (reference 8010-01-011-2649) and another lighter gray on the lower parts. Aircraft 64-1070, 64-1083, 65-0822, 65-0841, and 65-0873 had arrived with Hill Grey camouflage composed of two very different shades of gray, while aircraft 64-1069, 65-0835, and 65-0851, also having rounded, more modern noses, had a type of camouflage called Europe 1 in ash black and two shades of green. Fitted with a probe, the RF-4C became the only Air Force aircraft that could refuel via two methods: the flight

RF-4C 64-1070 with the colors of the USAF and *Hill Grey* camouflage shortly after arriving in Torrejón. It was one of eight ex-165 TRS/123 TRW Kentucky ANG aircraft. Here it is CR.12-46, January 1989. (José Terol)

Returning from the flyover at Armed Forces Day, CR.12-53—presently retired from service—heads toward the parking area at Torrejón, 10-12-1989. (Roberto Yáñez)

boom (a moveable tube) and the drogue and probe (a hose and probe).

At the same time, Ala 12 celebrated 20,000 flight hours of the F/RF-4C without any accidents. The last accident had happened six years previously. This is undoubtedly a good safety record, especially considering the age of the aircraft.

As the reconnaissance system for the EF-18 that met the requirements of the SARA (Advanced System of Aerial Reconnaissance) ended up being cancelled, it was decided to strengthen the capacity of the 123rd Squadron by acquiring some RF-4Cs, but with better equipment. Following this, six aircraft of the 192 RS *High Rollers*, 152 TRG, Nevada ANG, arrived in Torrejón: four in October 1995 and two in November. Transferred by ANG crews and still bearing the USAF livery in two shades of gray, they joined the eight others in service in the 123rd Squadron.

Returning from a very low altitude mission and probably due to an emergency, the pilot of CR.12-47 is forced to carry out fuel dumping to reduce the weight of the aircraft before its imminent landing. The trails produced by the fuel coming from the wing tanks accentuate the sensation of the aircraft's speed. (José Terol – Air Force press office)

CR.12-59 has recently landed, as can be seen by the activated brake chutes. As well as the fixed though detachable arm, it carried the tank of another aircraft under its left wing. The lens of the KS-87 camera can be seen through the nose window. (Air Force press office)

CR.12-57 carries out a turn, showing off the fairing of the front niches of the Sparrow missiles which, as well as showing off the shape of the Phantom, allow it to reach one more Mach point. Also visible is the arrangement of the nose windows and the LAU-7/A launcher, which allow the two Sidewinders to be fitted (1-25-2000). (Alberto Pina)

These RF-4Cs came with the most modern navigation and tactical reconnaissance equipment, such as the AN/APQ-172 radar, with terrain-following air-to-land mode and capable of carrying out full time missions at programmed altitudes; and AGL (above ground level) between 67m and 670m (200 feet and 2,000 feet). They also had secondary air-to-air capacity, the AN/ALR-46 radar warning receiver system, a weapons launching system, and NWDS computerized inertial navigation system. For defense, they carry AN/ALE-40 chaff and flare dispensers and can carry two Sidewinder AIM-9Ls. As far as budgets allow, the Air Force is incorporating these improvements into the rest of the CR.12s.

In addition to the camera equipment of the previous eight RF-4Cs, KA-91s were added: a high-altitude camera with an 18-inch lens that allows for stand-off operations, meaning outside the radius of enemy defenses at an altitude of 11,600m (35,000ft).

Nowadays, at the same time the Mod/IRAN is being carried out, the aircraft are also painted in the standard two shades of gray—darker on the upper parts and lighter on the lower parts—and all of them are fitted with in-flight refueling.

Epilogue

As the experiences of the recent conflicts in Europe have shown, the Air Force should obtain some ECM pods for carrying out tactical reconnaissance. On the other hand, the safety of the crews cannot be guaranteed and neither can the success of the operations.

For the RF-4C, the end of their operational life is approaching. Two of them were retired at the end of 1999 and their replacements should arrive soon. The solution given will affect their successor, in all probability the F-18.

Almost from its creation, the 123rd Squadron has participated not only in Air Force exercises, but also in exchanges with reconnaissance squadrons from other air forces in NATO countries. The first took place in the summer of 1990, with AG 51 of Bremgarten; then with the RF-4E; and then, in October 1999, with Escadron ERS 1/91, Mirage IVR. At the same time, groups of

The wheels have just touched down. In a moment, the orange-colored parachute will float behind CR.12-57, shortening its landing run considerably. The Visual Low-Altitude mission has finished. Torrejón, 1-25-2000. (Alberto Pina)

CR.12-57/12-66, showing the recently painted insignias of the Air Force. This is one of the six ex-192 RS Nevada ANG aircraft that were delivered to Ala 12 in October 1995 that joined the eight from the 123rd Squadron. Torrejón, 12-28-1995. (Gonzalo Ávila

Spanish pilots have been to Leck to train in the simulator there and have spent a week in Larissa, Greece, home of the 348 Mira Matia—fitted with RF-4E—where there is another simulator. Others passed some weeks in USAF units that have RF-4Cs, mainly the 192 RS, Nevada ANG. Members of this unit were also guests of the 123rd for similar periods of time.

The 123rd Squadron has also participated in multi-national exercises, including *Strong Resolve*, in Norway in 1995, and *Sirio 97*, a multi-national exercise in Spain during which the C3 system was evaluated.

Counting the last six RF-4Cs, the number of Phantom IIs delivered to the Air Force comes to fifty-eight. The life of these aircraft in Spain is coming to an end. Despite this, even on the ground, these old warriors still engender a great deal of respect.

◀ The second shift of the daytime operators is about to begin. The aircraft that are going to participate are on the line. In CR.12-54/12-63, it can be seen that part of the exterior pipes of the in-flight refueling arm is unpainted because it has been recently installed. Torrejón, 1-25-2000. (Gonzalo Ávila)

▼ CR.12-51, radio code *Titan 11* and painted one shade of gray all over, is photographed when landing at CASA-Getafe, 7-7-1995. (Roberto Yáñez)

C12-19
121-10
RESCUE
© GAVILA 1-00

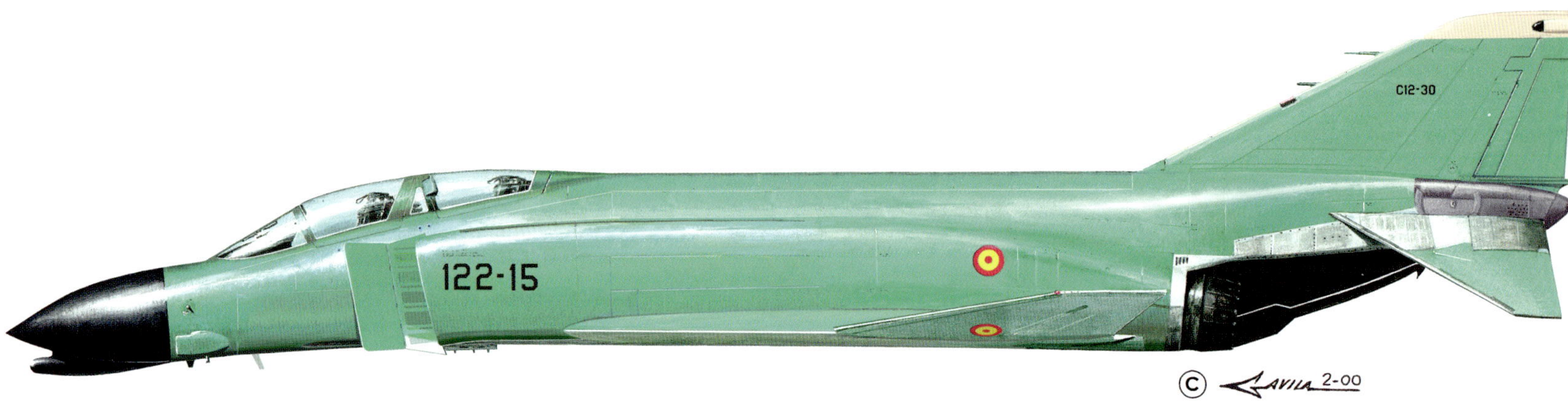
C12-30
122-15
© GAVILA 2-00

C12-19
12-33
RESCUE
© GAVILA 1-00

CR12-50
12-59
© AVILA 1-00

CR12-57
12-66
© AVILA 1-00

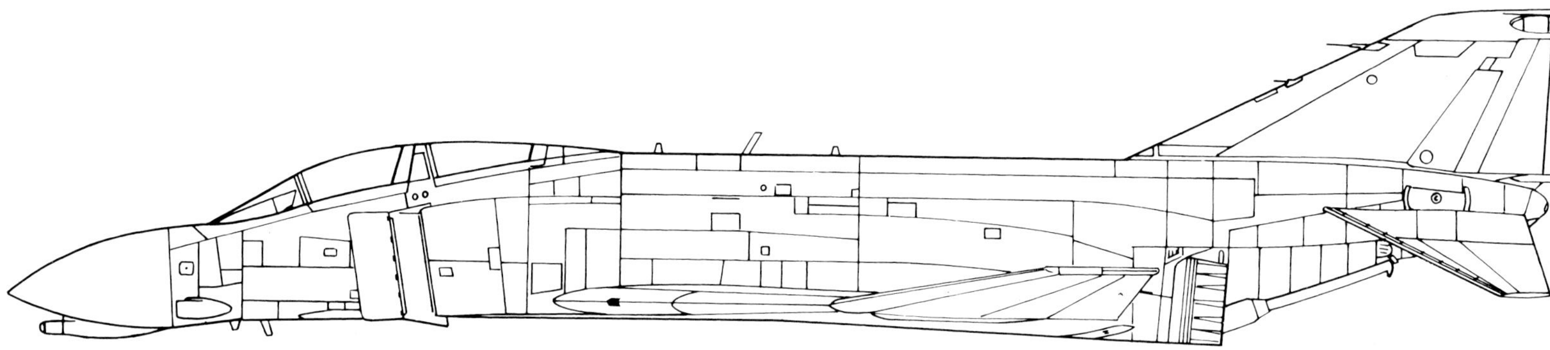

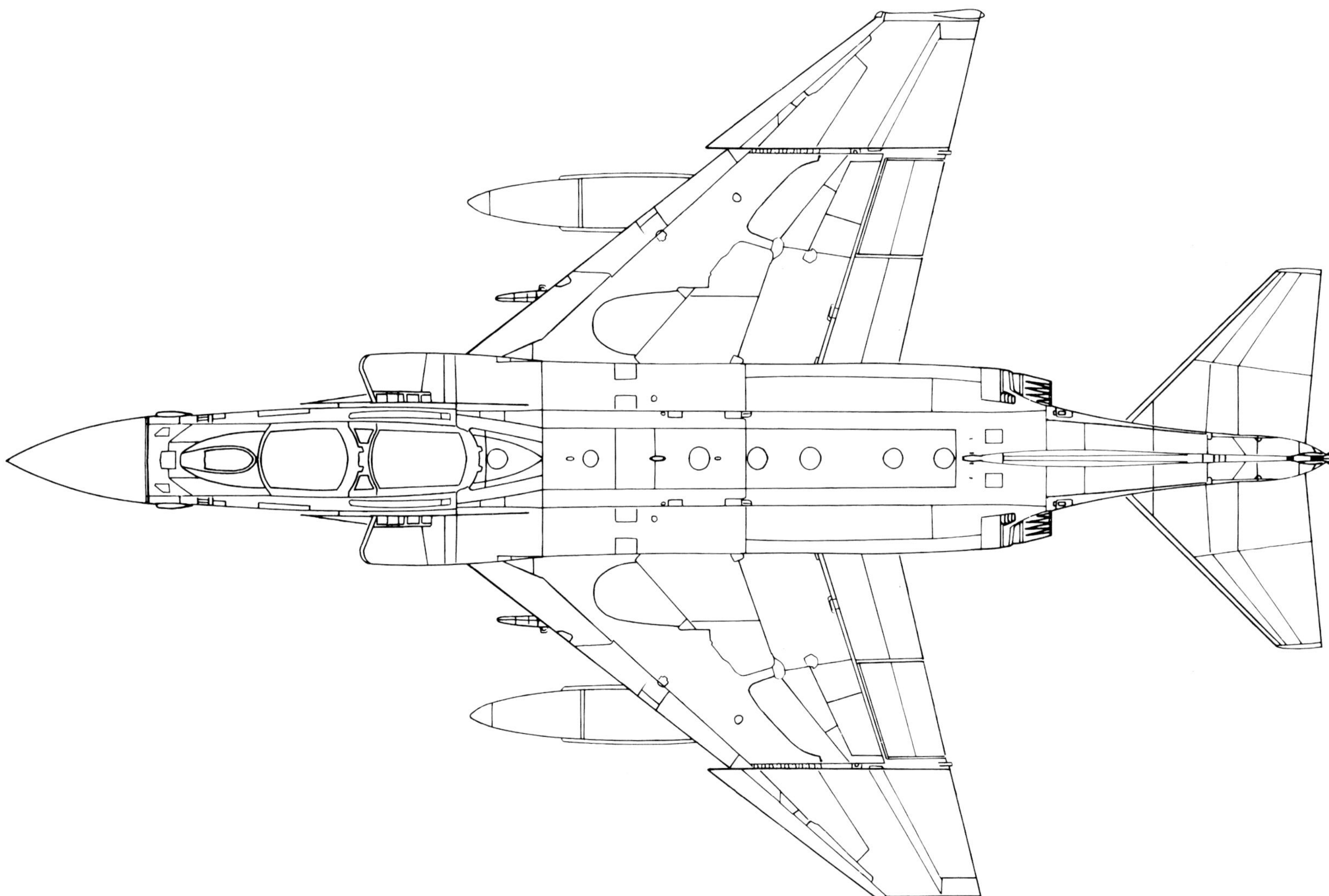

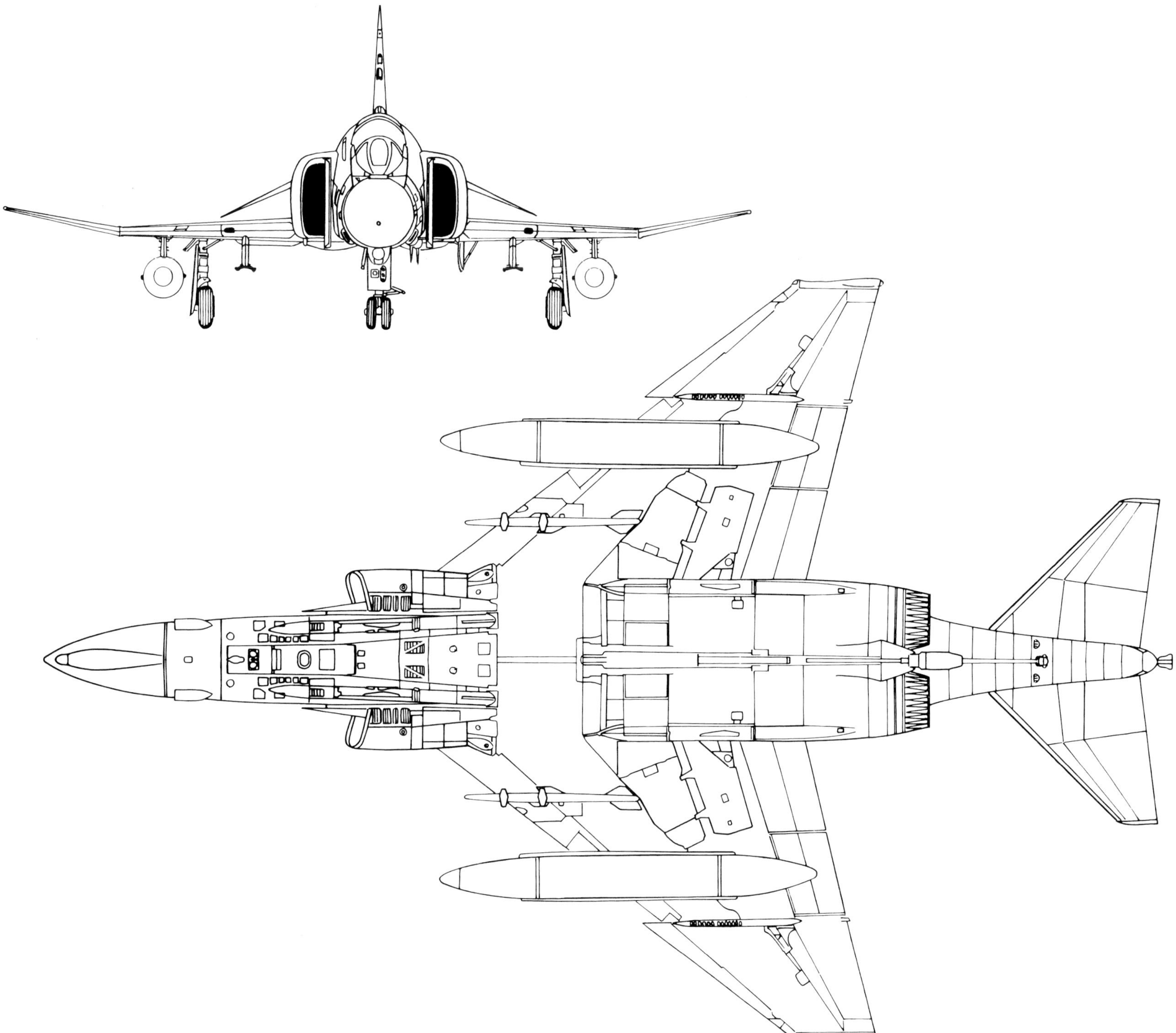

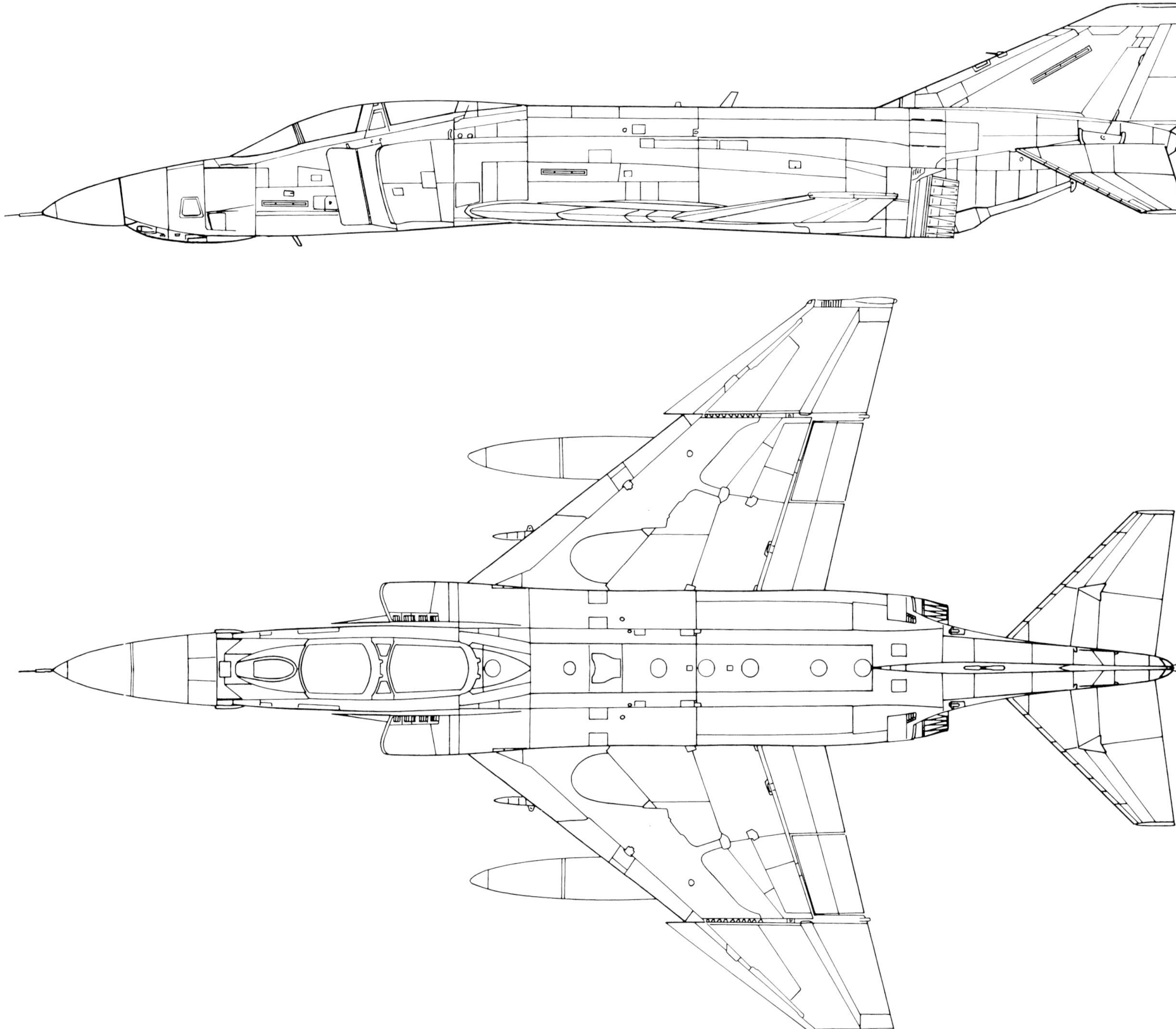

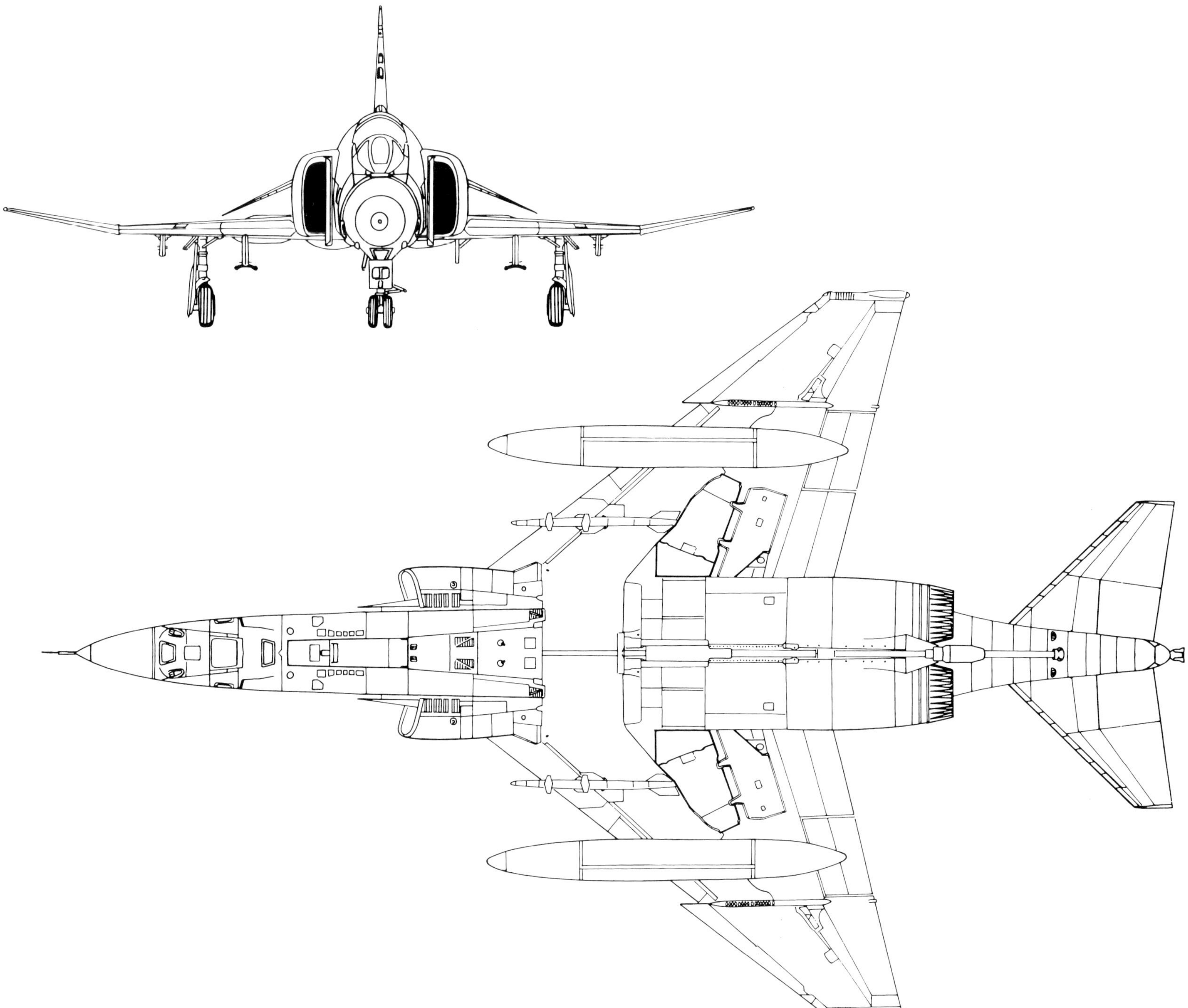

Air Force F-4C Phantom II

Spanish Military Registration Number	USAF Serial Number	Date of Delivery	Retirement Date	Unit Codes	Previous Allocation
C.12-01	64-884	7.06.71	20.07.78	121-01	92 TFS/81 TFW
C.12-02	64-900A	24.06.71	20.02.89	121-02, 122-01, 12-01 Mon.	92 TFS/81 TFW
C.12-03	64-903	18.06.71	20.02.89	121 03, 121 02,	92 TFS/81 TFW
C.12-04	64-909	6.07.71	20.02.89	121-04, 122-02,	92 TFS/81 TFW
C.12-05	64-906	22.07.71	28.11.73	121 05, 121-03,	92 TFS/81 TFW
C.12-06	64-886A	3.08.71	7.02.85	121-06, 122-03,	92 TFS/81 TFW
C.12-07	64-920A	16.09.71	20.02.89	121 07, 121 04,	91 TFS/81 TFW
C.12-08	64-925A	21.10.71	20.02.89	121-08, 122-04,	92 TFS/81 TFW
C.12-09	64-867	4.11.71	11.03.91	121-09, 121 05, 12-06,	91 TFS/81 TFW
C.12-10	64-895	5.11.71	11.03.91	121-10, 122-05, 12-07	92 TFS/81 TFW
C.12-11	64-871	11.11.71	20.02.89	121 11, 121 06,	92 TFS/81 TFW
C.12-12	64-846	23.11.71	20.02.89	121 12, 122-06,	91 TFS/81 TFW
C.12-13	64-813	1.12.71	7.05.79	121 13, 121-07,	91 TFS/81 TFW
C.12-14	64-850	20.12.71	11.03.91	121-14, 122-07,	91 TFS/81 TFW
C.12-15	64-886	3.01.72	20.02.89	121-15, 121 08, 12-11	92 TFS/81 TFW
C.12-16	64-868	12.01.72	20.02.89	121-16, 122-08, 12-12	92 TFS/81 TFW
C.12-17	64-853A	24.01.72	20.02.89	121-17, 121 09,	91 TFS/81 TFW
C.12-18	64-854A	14.02.72	20.02.89	121 18, 122-09, 12-14,	91 TFS/81 TFW
C.12-19	64-872	18.02.72	11.03.91	121-19, 122-01, 121 10, 12-15	92 TFS/81 TFW
C.12-20	64-855	1.03.72	11.03.91	121-20, 122-02, 122-10	91 TFS/81 TFW
C.12-21	64-857	24.03.72	14.10.77	121-21, 122-03, 121 11	91 TFS/81 TFW
C.12-22	64-924	3.03.72	20.02.89	121-22, 122-04, 122-11, 12-17	91 TFS/81 TFW
C.12-23	64-877	22.03.72	20.02.89	121-23, 122-05, 121 12, 12-18	92 TFS/81 TFW
C.12-24	64-894	28.03.72	4.05.84	121-24, 122-06, 122-12	91 TFS/81 TFW
C.12-25	64-881	11.04.72	14.02.75	121-13	92 TFS/81 TFW
C.12-26	64-861A	8.05.72	20.02.89	122-13	91 TFS/81 TFW
C.12-27	64-862A	26.05.72	20.02.89	121 14	91 TFS/81 TFW
C.12-28	64-880A	31.05.72	20.02.89	122-14	92 TFS/81 TFW
C.12-29	64-858A	15.06.72	20.02.89	121 15, 12-22	91 TFS/81 TFW
C.12-30	64-878A	22.06.72	20.02.89	122-15	91 TFS/81 TFW
C.12-31	64-859	30.06.72	20.02.89	121 16	91 TFS/81 TFW
C.12-32	64-856A	17.07.72	20.02.89	122-16	91 TFS/81 TFW
C.12-33	64-887A	17.07.72	20.02.89	121 17, 12-33	92 TFS/81 TFW
C.12-34	64-907A	27.07.72	20.02.89	122-17	92 TFS/81 TFW
C.12-35	64-870A	19.09.72	25.04.83	121 18	91 TFS/81 TFW
C.12-36	64-864	28.09.72	20.02.89	122-18	91 TFS/81 TFW
C.12-37	64-820	10.07.78	11.03.91	12-29	311 TFTS/58 TFTW
C.12-38	64-882	3.08.78	20.02.89	----	310 TFTS/58 TFTW
C.12-39	64-892	3.08.78	20.02.89	12-31	310 TFTS/58 TFTW
C.12-40	64-896A	24.07.78	20.02.89	12-32	311 TFTS/58 TFTW

Air Force RF-4C Phantom II

Spanish Military Registration Number	USAF Serial Number	Date of Delivery	Retirement Date	Unit Codes	Previous Allocation
CR.12-41	65-936	31.10.78	20.02.89	----	62 TRS/363 TRW
CR.12-42	65-937	13.11.78	11.03.91	12-51	62 TRS/363 TRW
CR.12-43	65-938	17.11.78	20.02.89	----	18 TRS/363 TRW
CR.12-44	65-943	13.11.78	20.02.89	----	18 TRS/363 TRW
CR.12-45	64-1069	12.01.89		12-54	165 TRS/123 TRW
CR.12-46	64-1070	12.01.89		12-55	165 TRS/123 TRW
CR.12-47	64-1083	12.01.89		12-56	165 TRS/123 TRW
CR.12-48	65-822	12.01.89		12-57	165 TRS/123 TRW
CR.12-49	65-835	12.01.89		12-58	165 TRS/123 TRW
CR.12-50	65-841	12.01.89		12-59	165 TRS/123 TRW
CR.12-51	65-851	12.01.89		12-60	165 TRS/123 TRW
CR.12-52	65-873	12.01.89		12-61	165 TRS/123 TRW
CR.12-53	64-1006	26.10.95	(*)	12-62	192 TRS/152 TRG
CR.12-54	64-1039	14.11.95		12-63	192 TRS/152 TRG
CR.12-55	65-823	14.11.95		12-64	192 TRS/152 TRG
CR.12-56	65-864	26.10.95		12-65	192 TRS/152 TRG
CR.12-57	65-876	26.10.95		12-66	192 TRS/152 TRG
CR.12-58	65-897	26.10.95	(*)	12-67	192 TRS/152 TRG

(*) Retired from service at the end of 1999, but without a retirement date. CR.12-58 received a tremendous blow to the nose when it hit a very large bird.

Phantom II F/RF-4C:

MAIN PANEL AREA
(BEFORE TO 1F-4-1500)

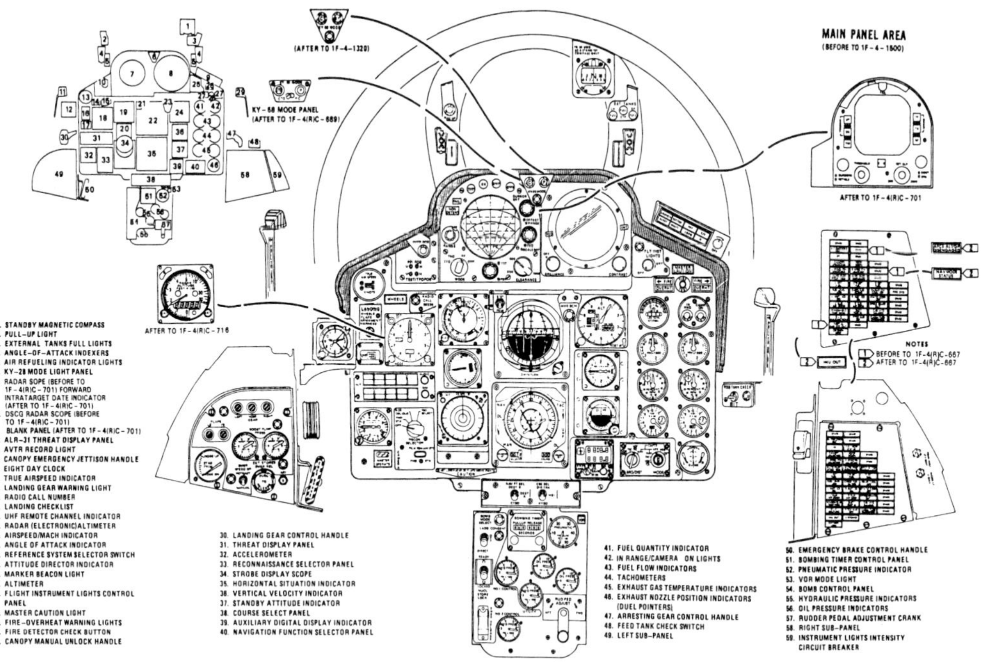

1. STANDBY MAGNETIC COMPASS
2. PULL-UP LIGHT
3. EXTERNAL TANKS FULL LIGHTS
4. ANGLE-OF-ATTACK INDEXERS
5. AIR REFUELING INDICATOR LIGHTS
6. KY-28 MODE LIGHT PANEL
7. RADAR SOPE (BEFORE TO 1F-4(R)C-701) FORWARD INTRATARGET DATE INDICATOR (AFTER TO 1F-4(R)C-701)
8. DSCG RADAR SCOPE (BEFORE TO 1F-4(R)C-701) BLANK PANEL (AFTER TO 1F-4(R)C-701)
9. ALR-31 THREAT DISPLAY PANEL
10. AVTR RECORD LIGHT
11. CANOPY EMERGENCY JETTISON HANDLE
12. EIGHT DAY CLOCK
13. TRUE AIRSPEED INDICATOR
14. LANDING GEAR WARNING LIGHT
15. RADIO CALL NUMBER
16. LANDING CHECKLIST
17. UHF REMOTE CHANNEL INDICATOR
18. RADAR (ELECTRONIC)ALTIMETER
19. AIRSPEED/MACH INDICATOR
20. ANGLE OF ATTACK INDICATOR
21. REFERENCE SYSTEM SELECTOR SWITCH
22. ATTITUDE DIRECTOR INDICATOR
23. MARKER BEACON LIGHT
24. ALTIMETER
25. FLIGHT INSTRUMENT LIGHTS CONTROL PANEL
26. MASTER CAUTION LIGHT
27. FIRE-OVERHEAT WARNING LIGHTS
28. FIRE DETECTOR CHECK BUTTON
29. CANOPY MANUAL UNLOCK HANDLE
30. LANDING GEAR CONTROL HANDLE
31. THREAT DISPLAY PANEL
32. ACCELEROMETER
33. RECONNAISSANCE SELECTOR PANEL
34. STROBE DISPLAY SCOPE
35. HORIZONTAL SITUATION INDICATOR
36. VERTICAL VELOCITY INDICATOR
37. STANDBY ATTITUDE INDICATOR
38. COURSE SELECT PANEL
39. AUXILIARY DIGITAL DISPLAY INDICATOR
40. NAVIGATION FUNCTION SELECTOR PANEL
41. FUEL QUANTITY INDICATOR
42. IN RANGE/CAMERA ON LIGHTS
43. FUEL FLOW INDICATORS
44. TACHOMETERS
45. EXHAUST GAS TEMPERATURE INDICATORS
46. EXHAUST NOZZLE POSITION INDICATORS (DUEL POINTERS)
47. ARRESTING GEAR CONTROL HANDLE
48. FEED TANK CHECK SWITCH
49. LEFT SUB-PANEL
50. EMERGENCY BRAKE CONTROL HANDLE
51. BOMBING TIMER CONTROL PANEL
52. PNEUMATIC PRESSURE INDICATOR
53. VOR MODE LIGHT
54. BOMB CONTROL PANEL
55. HYDRAULIC PRESSURE INDICATORS
56. OIL PRESSURE INDICATORS
57. RUDDER PEDAL ADJUSTMENT CRANK
58. RIGHT SUB-PANEL
59. INSTRUMENT LIGHTS INTENSITY CIRCUIT BREAKER

LEFT CONSOLE AREA

1. LEFT UTILITY PANEL
2. OXYGEN CONTROL PANEL
3. ENGINE CONTROL PANEL (INBOARD)
4. DRAG CHUTE CONTROL HANDLE
5. VOR/ILS CONTROL PANEL
6. AFCS CONTROL PANEL
7. INTERCOM SYSTEM CONTROL PANEL
8. COMMUNICATION SELECTOR PANEL
9. BLANK PANEL
10. ANTI-G SUIT CONTROL VALVE
11. ARMAMENT SAFETY OVERRIDE SWITCH
12. BLANK PANEL
13. KY-28 CONTROL PANEL
14. FUEL CONTROL PANEL
15. RAM AIR TURBINE CONTROL HANDLE
16. CANOPY CONTROL SELECTOR
17. WING FLAP CONTROL PANEL
18. EJECT LIGHT/SWITCH
19. ENGINE CONTROL PANEL (OUTBOARD)
20. LANDING AND TAXI LIGHTS SWITCH
21. THROTTLES

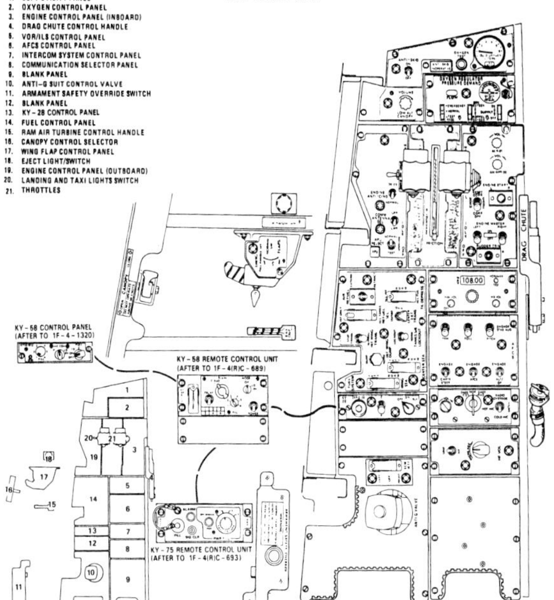

RIGHT CONSOLE AREA

FRONT COCKPIT

TYPICAL

WITH DMAS

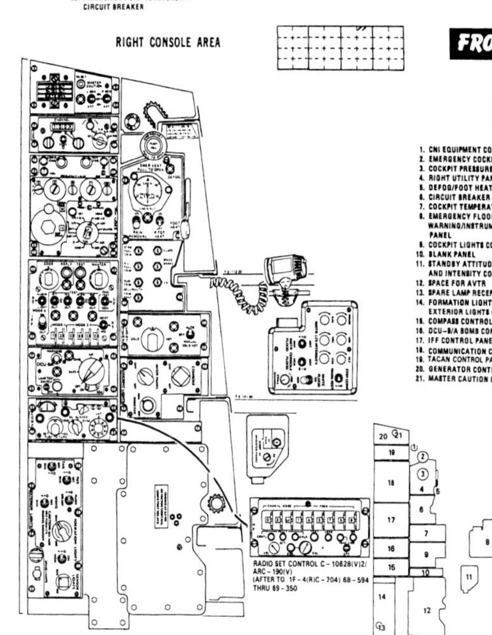

1. CNI EQUIPMENT COOLING RESET BUTTON
2. EMERGENCY COCKPIT VENT KNOB
3. COCKPIT PRESSURE INDICATOR
4. RIGHT UTILITY PANEL
5. DEFOG/FOOT HEAT CONTROL HANDLE
6. CIRCUIT BREAKER PANEL
7. COCKPIT TEMPERATURE CONTROL PANEL
8. EMERGENCY FLOOD LIGHTS/AURAL STALL WARNING/INSTRUMENT LIGHTS INTENSITY PANEL
9. COCKPIT LIGHTS CONTROL PANEL
10. BLANK PANEL
11. STANDBY ATTITUDE CIRCUIT BREAKER AND INTENSITY CONTROL PANEL
12. SPACE FOR AVTR
13. SPARE LAMP RECEPTACLE
14. FORMATION LIGHTS CONTROL PANEL EXTERIOR LIGHTS CONTROL PANEL
15. COMPASS CONTROL PANEL
16. DCU-9/A BOMB CONTROL MONITOR PANEL
17. IFF CONTROL PANEL
18. COMMUNICATION CONTROL PANEL
19. TACAN CONTROL PANEL
20. GENERATOR CONTROL PANEL
21. MASTER CAUTION LIGHT RESET BUTTON

The rear cabin of the F-4C was the office of the OA (Arms Operator). In here there is the screen of the Westinghouse APQ-100 radar, the controls of the weapons launch computer, the timers, the radios, the navigation equipment, and electronic warfare equipment. In the RF-4Cs, there were also the camera controls. Some of the instruments in the upper part were disassembled for training missions so that the instructor, who was in the rear seat, was able to see something when it was time to land. (Pere Redón)

F/RF-4C: Technical Specifications

Dimensions

Length	18.47m [60.6ft] (F-4C) 19.14m [63.8ft] (RF-4C)
Wing span	11.71m [38.42ft]
Height	5.03m [16.50ft]
Wing area	49.23m² [530ft²]

Weight

Empty weight:	12,823kg [28,270lbs]
Maximum take-off weight	26,303kg [57.988lbs]

Speed

Cruising speed	945km/h [587.2mph]
Maximum speed	2,548km/h [1,583mph] at 14,721m [48,297ft] (Mach 2.4) 1,472km/h [914.66mph] at sea level (Mach 1.2)
Climb	14.721m/m [48.3ft/min]
Ceiling	18,104m [59,396ft]

Radius of action

with 2,700kg [5,952lbs]	1,287km [800 miles] (at 675km/h [419 mph])
without refueling:	3,700km [2,299 miles] (flight in ferry transfer)

Motor

Two General Electric J79-GE-15 of 4,944kgp each (7,711kgp with afterburner)

Armament

Four AIM-7E Sparrow III
Four AIM-9L Sidewinder and
7,500kg [16,535lbs] defensive load
Two AIM-9L Sidewinder for
self defense (RF-4C)

Other (RF-4C)

Aerial photography	3 Cameras: 2 oblique 1 central panoramic

Collection of arms for a Phantom II F-4C, with up to 18 LAU-3A launchers capable of storing 19 2.75-inch rockets in clusters of three fitted in the four underwing supports and two others located under the belly of the aircraft. In the foreground is the the SUU-16/A cannon pod and four Sparrow missiles. Torrejón air base, November 1984. (Pere Redón)

The lens of the versatile Hycon KS-87 camera, capable of operating day and night at low and high altitude, is visible through the side window of the nose of CR.12-48. The aircraft is still without the in-flight fueling system and is painted with a camouflage of two very different shades of gray. The serial numbers of the fourteen RF-4Cs of the 123rd Squadron are applied in the same order as their USAF serial numbers. (MALOG)

Despite the generalized application of the gray camouflage to Spanish aircraft, the use of different shades offers a superior capacity for disguise. CR.12-50/12-49 and CR.12-56/12-65, with both liveries, are on a training flight. (MALOG)

On a squadron exchange, Phantoms CR.12-45, -48, -55, and -58 of the 123rd Squadron fly in formation over the Gascogne countryside, together with the Mirage IVR AJ and AX of the Escadron de Reconnaisance Strategique 1/91 *Gascogne*, September 1999. (123rd Squadron)